Shamel Hundred
in old picture postcards

by D.S. Worsdale

European Library   ZALTBOMMEL/THE NETHERLANDS

GB ISBN 90 288 6088 6/ CIP
© 1995 European Library – Zaltbommel/The Netherlands

No part of this book may be reproduced in any form, by print, photoprint, microfilm or any other means, without written permission from the publisher.

Introduction

The 'Hundred' became established in medieval times as a convenient way of assessing and collecting taxes. It was made up of one hundred 'Hides'. A hide was that quantity of land capable of supporting the life of a family for one year and might have varied (according to some sources) between two acres and 120 acres in size. In effect, the hide was both the acreage unit and the family unit. Hides were gathered in a variety of numbers under the control of a 'Manor' and these were grouped together to number one hundred hides or thereabouts, forming the Hundred. The Hundred of Shamel (the Domesday record spells it Essamele and other records spell it Seamele) consisted, according to Hasted, the Kent historian, of the manors of Cobham, Shorne, Halling (Hallinger), Cuxton (Coclestane), Wicham, Beresse, Henhurst and Haydon (the Mount), Roundall (or Randall), Chalk (east and west), Beccles, Raynehurst and Tymberwood, Denton, Merston (now lost), Higham, Great Okeley, Higham Ridgeway, Cliffe, Burycourt (Perrycourt), Molland, Cardons, Mortimers, Cooling (Couling), New Barn and others which were no more than large farms. They frequently changed hands, often through marriage, but mainly through property deals. Edward Hasted produced the second edition of his survey of Kent between 1797 and 1801.

Throughout the whole of the Hundred there can be found evidence of, and the remains of ancient and old civilisations. The ancient routes like the Pilgrim's Way was in use centuries before Chaucer gave us his Canterbury Tales. The Sarson Stones scattered along the road in Cobham were thought to have been stationed around an ancient communal grave in Battle Street. At Cooling an excavated mound revealed a Roman and early British industrial site of the earliest centuries A.D. At Cuxton, there has been found evidence of ancient man in the form of axeheads and other implements and a Roman villa once stood in the churchyard.

Halling, too, can boast of the discovery of a skeleton of the Neolithic age. Higham has, nearby, the remains of a Saxon burial ground and fairly significant Roman remains. In Chalk are the remains of a Roman cellar, part of a villa which contained evidence that the Romans had slaves. One who lived in this cellar left his mark on a pot – 'Felix'. Industry seems to have flourished mainly in the southern parishes alongside the river Medway. The production of cement was thriving in the late nineteenth century in both Halling and Cuxton and survives in Halling to this day. Cliffe also in the same period had cement producers, the first in Kent, but an explosives factory was already in production. Otherwise, agriculture and work connected with the rural nature of the area especially in support of the large houses and estate management, continued at Cobham Hall, at Higham's Great Hermitage, at Knowle, at Great Okeley and Mockbeggar. Hops are grown, fewer these days, and fruit. Some of the personalities and events associated with the Hundred of Shamel are included in the following lines. Travelling from Thames' side to the river Medway, St. Helen's Church at Cliffe can boast of a priest's room over the porch (which makes the entrance very dark) and John Wesley's grandfather, Samuel Annersley, rector at St. Helen's about 1640, gave an hour glass for the timing of the sermons; the bracket it rested on is still there. Arthur Broome, a curate, who came to the parish in 1812, was responsible for calling the first meeting of those interested in animal welfare which finally led to the formation of the RSPCA. In 1868, shortly after the first cement factory started working, General Gordon, who was in charge of the troops stationed at the fort, complained that fumes from the kilns were affecting the troops' health. At Cobham the church of Saint Mary Magdalene contains an exceptional collection of 'brasses' including memorials to the families whose 'seat' was at the Hall; Cobham, Brookes Lennox and

Darnley. The Hall in its present form was started in 1584 but was extensively altered in the seventeenth century and many of these alterations can be seen today. Behind the church is the 'College' which is illustrated in the text. Cooling Castle has associations with John Oldcastle, the Lollard leader in 1409. The partly Norman church is now on the redundant list. Cuxton has a church, St. Michael's and All Angels, which faces south east instead of east and a rhyme says: 'He that would see a church miswent, let him go to Cocklestane in Kent.' This is because the chancel is set slightly out of alignment when looking down the nave. In days past, the bishops of Rochester had their palace alongside the river at Halling, but now only a part of one wall remains. At Higham, Charles Dickens lived a Gads Hill Place and Charles Larkin's monument stands on Telegraph Hill, both close to the famous Sir John Falstaff Inn. Shorne's Butchers Hill, where stands the 'Rose and Crown' and nearby its pretty post office, has a distant view of the Thames – one of the most picturesque villages in Kent.

The collection is roughly divided as follows: Important Houses, Communications, Industry, Social conditions, Rural activities, Leisure and Sport, and Churches.

Acknowledgements and thanks are due to: Derek Church for items from his extensive collection on Cuxton; Ted Gowers for items for his extensive collection on Halling; Mick Scott for items from his extensive collection on Cliffe and elsewhere; Higham W.I./Roger and Karen Blyth, of 'The Sir John Falstaff' Inn; Mrs. Lynda Styles for typing and my wife, Margaret, for her patience and loss of company.

1   Cobham Hall as it is seen today was started in 1584 by William Brookland, and is one of the most spendid Tudor mansions in the country. There have been considerable alterations; in 1672 a new central block and the west front were built and the interior was transformed by James Wyatt's work. False Tudor additions were made at various times throughout the eighteenth century. The Hall is now in the hands of the Westwood Educational Trust and is a girls' school.

2   Gads Hill Place was once the residence of Charles Dickens. It appears that he had always hoped for the opportunity to acquire it and it finally came his way in 1856 and he was able to purchase it for £1,790. In the garden, at one time, stood a 'Swiss' style chalet in which it is said Dickens would spend time writing. It is reported that Dickens spent a fair slice of his life in this area, first at Chatham and then Gads Hill and thereby acquired the background for some of his works as in Great Expectations. The chalet was removed from the garden here and was re-erected in the grounds of Eastgate, Rochester, now a Dickensian museum. Dickens built a tunnel between the garden and the house. The house is now a girls' school.

3   This postcard, dated 1915 shows the Rectory at Cliffe, a building of some antiquity, as seen in this picture. There is a more modern frontage to it. The living here in the seventeenth century was worth £300 and described as 'one of the prizes of the Church'. This should not be entirely surprising when on reflection it is realised that Cliffe in earlier centuries was an important place, having hosted synods and in due course housed at the Rectory, two Chancellors of the Exchequer, two archbishops, three deans and eleven archdeacons; Nicholas Heath, Bishop of Rochester and Archbishop of Worcester. Samuel Annerley was appointed Lord Privy Seal in 1649. His daughter, Anne, married the Reverend Samuel Wesley, who was the father of John Wesley, founder of the Wesleyans. These are but a few of those clerics who at one time or another occupied the Rectory at Cliffe.

4   This postcard of Cooling Castle was dated 1905 and adressed to someone in Croydon. Lord John Cobham built the castle following permission granted by the King in February 1381. At this time, Cobham was in charge of the defence of Kent but a successful raid by the French and Spanish up to Gravesend persuaded the King that some solid defence was necessary. The two remaining towers shown here were built by Thomas Crump of Maidstone and the walls are exceptionally thick. They are 'half-drums'. The site is now owned by the Bridge Wardens of Rochester.

5   The Knowle was built by Reverend Joseph Hindle in about 1857. He had previously lived at Gads Hill Place during his incumbency as vicar at Higham and when Charles Dickens bought it in 1856 the new vicarage, Knowle, was not complete. Dickens allowed him to stay until he could move into his new premises. Hindle was obviously a wealthy man and spent a lot of his wealth on his church. He died in 1874 and is buried in a vault in St. Mary's church.

6   This postcard, dated 1915, shows the entrance to Cobham Park and the old Lodge. The decorative thatching is worthy of note. This view was lost when the roads were re-routed to accommodate the advent of the new road system and the 'feeder' to the A2/M2.

7   The Great Hermitage was one of the important houses of the area from 1736 to 1949 – for 213 years, during which time apart from being a gentleman's residence, it was a monastery occupied by Belgian monks, a wartime hospital, a country club and a kennels. It was a 56-room mansion built for Sir Francis Head on what is now known as Hermitage Road. After the death of Lady Head in the latter years of the eighteenth century, a Mrs. Pickersgill-Cunliffe occupied it. She, at one time, employed a large household staff to the benefit of the local population. She was followed by a Mr. Thomas Winch of the well-known family of solicitors and brewers. During the First World War the premises were used as a hospital. During alterations in August 1938 it caught fire but was left to burn itself out because of the difficulty of obtaining water. The site was redeveloped in 1949 and a smart, modern house of less pretentious proportions was built on the site.

8   This postcard, dated 1920, shows the house known as High Birch in Upper Bush, Cuxton. It is a Wealden type of timber framed building of traditional proportions. There are several similar examples in Kent. At one time it was divided into three cottages and Lord Darnley's gamekeepers lived at one end. The middle section was occupied by Lord Darn-ley's wood reeve. This house is very old and no-one appears to know exactly when it was built, however, it has now been returned to its original shape, although it is assumed that it will have an interior with modern appliances.

9   Further down the hillside sloping toward the Thames stands the Roman Catholic Chapel of St. Katherine. This is one of the few pre-reformation religious buildings remaining in catholic hands. It is presumed to be a thirteenth century building with a fifteenth century extension at the western end. Very little is known of its history except that in 1516 it was badly in need of repair. For some three hundred years it was used as a malthouse and then in 1890 it was bought and repaired by Mr. George Arnold, the Gravesend solicitor. It is now used by the Corpus Christi Carmelite Sisters. In the distance is the River Thames and before it Higham Marshes.

10   This postcard shows the Waterworks at Halling 'between the wars'. A large proportion of it was pulled down in 1912, some of it, I understand, remains in place. It stood a few yards above the County Primary School in Vicarage Lane (sheet TQ 663643). Behind the works are the remains of a deep quarry somewhat extensive in area. At one time, allotment gardens occupied a portion of the floor of the quarry.

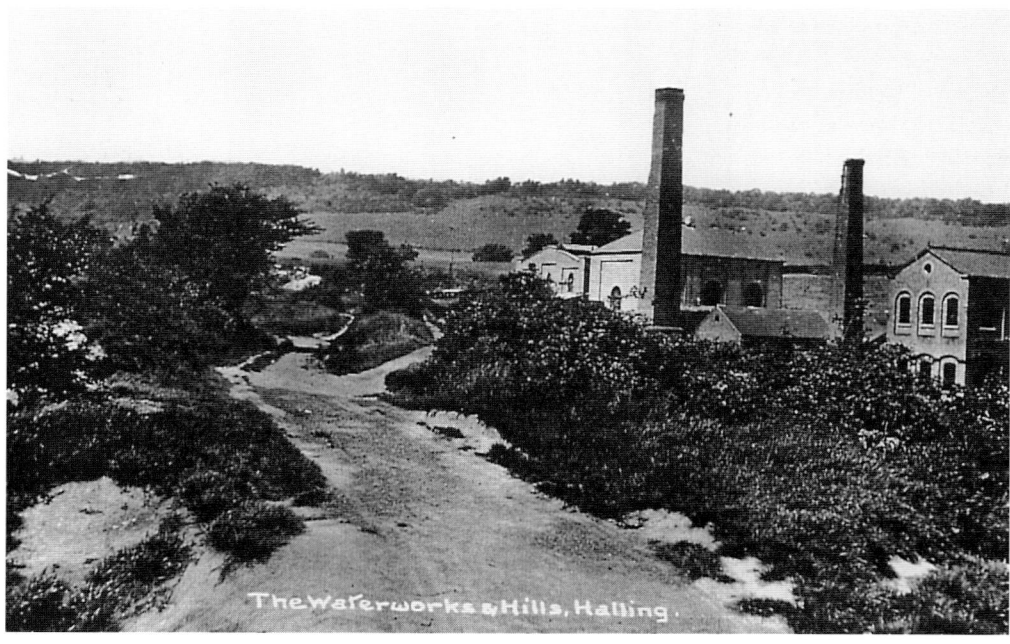

11 The Thames and Medway Canal was built between Strood and Gravesend and included a tunnel through the ridge above Frindsbury, to Higham. Problems abounded, especially in relation to the tides and a steam engine was used to pump water into the canal at critical periods; at one time a steam tug was employed to haul the barges through the tunnel. The canal was opened for traffic in May 1824 but twenty years later the shareholders were talking about converting the tunnel for use by a railway. In 1846, the waterway in the tunnel was filled in but the Higham/Gravesend section continued to work, if only for the carriage of farm manure which was unloaded at Higham Wharf. Nevertheless, the canal **was** used and for a period it provided picturesque scenes like this one.

12 'Billycan' Geary (standing) and Johnson Paris (sitting right) left armed service in the navy and joined 'Treacle' Mills, master of his barge. Mr. Mills found them particularly valuable for their knowledge of local coastal waters between the United Kingdom and the Channel ports. As a team they were well-known on the river.

13   Here is a picture of Whornes Place before 1926. The end of the old barn, the 'stepped' wall can be seen; it was demolished in 1926 and other buildings which can be seen here have, in 1995, disappeared. Most of the original Whornes Place was built by Sir William Whorne, Lord Mayor of London in 1487. The old granary had been converted into a farmhouse and still remains. At the end of the nineteenth century the property had been taken over by the cement industry and finally by Trechmann Weekes & Co., whose chimneys and factory sheds can be seen through the old arch.

14 This is a postcard showing Whornes Place some time in the 1920's. It is referred to elsewhere, but here the end of the great barn can be seen more clearly and the gable end of the dormer window can be seen to reflect the style of construction in the barn. The ivy covered porch can be seen to this day (1995, even in a dilapidated condition) but with restoration projected it is hoped that this building can be preserved. Mr 'Milky Bill' Masson is standing on the pavement.

15 This picture of the 1911 strike at Trechmann Weekes & Co's works shows the pickets at the Whornes Place entrance under the arch. Left to right are Mr. Manley, 'Molly' Homewood, Joe Manley, Tom Bowles, 'Jumper' Bonnywell, Bill Brown, Mr. Pooley and Walter Rule. The old cowshed and stables and the tall chimneys of the factory can be seen in the background. Fortunately, the strike did not last for very long but caused, as usual in those days, a lot of local hardship for the families involved.

16   As in any manufacturing business, workers would 'break' occasionally to relax and have just a little fun. Here the workers are holding a mock wedding. Jack Large, in the middle of the group with his 'bride' is attended by the 'bridesmaids', some of whom have managed to find appropriate head-gear. Jack Large was a cripple and, like others who were disabled in some way, was employed as a sack mender. The girls were employed to lift the wicker baskets from the aerial ropeway. At certain times of the year conditions underfoot were apalling and only old, worn clothing was used for work.

17   Here is Ernie (Alley) Saunders who drove one of the several horses and carts used for general work around the cement works at Cuxton and for the delivery of cement in the local area. This picture is interesting for it shows the 'cluster' of chimneys which were something of a landmark and also, in the background above Ernie's head, can just be seen two of the 'bottle' kilns which were used here in the manufacture of the cement. 'Chamber' kilns were also used. On one occasion 'Alley' Saunders was backing his horse and cart in the direction of the edge of the wharf and through lack of concentration, both cart and horse suddenly went backwards over the edge into thick mud. Both were rescued by crane.

18   This postcard is from a series of 'scenes from rural life' by Kent County Council and dated 1861. In that era such photographs were 'posed', as this one obviously is. The subjects' postures and apparel is echoed in the other pictures in the series and at least one of the characters can be 'spotted' elsewhere. The arch can be seen in the picture of the quadrangle of New Cobham College.

19 Also from the 'rural life' series, this is a scene from the imagination about rural (or country) life held by many; it probably holds a social comment as well. Here sit the old and the infirm while the young girl from the house has to fetch the water from the well. The lad would not have found the crutch very comfortable when taking the weight of his 'club' foot whilst walking.

20   Again from the 'rural life' series. The old fellow should have known better than to have attracted the attention of the lad sharpening the blade – OK! – the picture is posed and perhaps it was not intended that the handle of the stone should be turned. The old chap is recognisable from another picture. The shafts of a light carriage are protruding from shed.

21   This house appeared on a postcard dated 1909 in Cliffe. It shows Quickrells Farm House with Mrs. Lane standing at the door. The farm lands have gone – swallowed up by the housing development in the area which included, no doubt, the fire station which is situated next door. The house remains much as seen here quite near to the centre of the village.

22 Buckland is a small farming hamlet to the west of the B.2000, just a few yards from the railway line, here hidden in a cutting, which connects Thamesport (used to be BP refinery) on the Isle of Grain with the main line system. The horse being held here is either a 'Shire' or a 'Clydesdale'; either would have been used for work on the heavy soil in this area close to the Higham Marshes just along the road on the other side of the railway bridge.

23   Like most hop-pickers, this group had no doubt returned to the same farm they came to in the previous year and in the years before that also. The families and young children came as well, as seen in the picture, and learnt the traditional skills required by the work in those days and also of 'camping' out. This group, 'Sunday best hats and all', are obviously enjoying themselves, especially the two younger members who were probably 'missing' at school. They were at Upper Halling Court Farm, could it be Mr. Lingham looking over the bar?

24 When Rose's Mill was redeveloped after the 1920 storm damaged it beyond economic repair, it took on the appearance shown here. Thoughtfully, the miller C.J. Rose incorporated one of the old grindstones in the pathway. The vans are as can be seen, Fords of the early 1930's.

25   This windmill, known as Rose's Windmill, here as seen in 1904. The name appears to have come from one of the millers. Like the other great building in Hermitage Road, it was built by Sir Richard Head in 1760. Unusually, bread was baked on the premises and in this instance, specifically for the army at Chatham and it also ground corn for other farmers in the area. A great storm in 1920 seriously damaged the mill and all but the base and one floor was removed. The remains were turned into storage and when I passed a few weeks ago it looked as though part of the base was now a garage.

26   The Forge, the building furthest away in this picture, had probably been in this position since the middle of the sixteenth century. This picture, about 1900, shows two members of the family with long association with and work in, as blacksmiths. They are Mr. Clifton, blacksmith and Ian Smith, his striker. Two of the Clifton children also appear in the picture. The family moved out of the Forge in 1932; they had been there for 150 years. Forge Cottage, next door, has according to reports, changed little since 1900. The Forge has now virtually disappeared amongst the rubble.

27   Also from the rural life series of 1861, this young lady is obviously in need of some new footwear by 1995 standards but standing, as she is, at the door of one of the almshouses in New Cobham College, she well illustrates the poor of the time. The shape of the arch and the oval shape of the plate on the door can also be seen in the quadrangle scene. At one time the names of the villages of the main dedications were inscribed on the door-plates.

28   This scene, also from the series portraying rural life in 1861, shows the same dilapidated appearance of the porch of the refectory at Cobham New College as it appears in the card postmarked 1913. The same dilapidated appearance, but properly repaired and supported is evident in 1995. The cap-wearing chap is easily recognisable even without his pipe.

29   These are Dean Farm Cottages about 1910. This is a winter scene and from the comfort of a late twentieth century centrally heated home it is difficult (for me anyway) to imagine how difficult life would have been for the Baker family who had occupied one of the cottages at the time of the photo. In the background can be seen stacks of hop supports. The whole area of Upper Bush was used for hop growing.

30   At the time when this building was a row of cottages it was known as 'Clack Alley' and I can only surmise about the origin of this name! The picture was taken in 1904. This building was originally built in 1390 and was known as a 'hall' house. It is probably the oldest surviving building in Cuxton, apart from the church. After considerable renovation to return it to some semblance of its original shape and style it is now known as Barrow Hill House.

31   To the local population at least, Mockbeggar means orchards and fruit picking. But to others, those who lived in the big house, for instance, the two ladies shown here, it meant comfort, servants and elegant living, typical of the 'landed gentry' in the early part of the century. The actual date of this picture is not known but the two ladies were of the Cobb family who were and are estate agents and auctioneers. The house stands in Cliffe Road, partly in Frindsbury, partly in Higham and partly in Cliffe. It has been added to and altered considerably since the early Tudor period when it was first built.

32   Here is a group of senior pupils at the National School, Cuxton, in about 1900. The headmaster, Mr. Strickson, is on the right. The old National School building was demolished in 1964 but after being closed as a 'day school' it was, for a time, used as a Sunday school. The 'National School' was provided by the Church of England and its daily act of worship was usually 'taken' by the vicar. In this picture, the 'stiff' collars were typically worn by choir boys. They were very uncomfortable to wear. If one raised one's shoulders one was liable to cut the throat or be decapitated. If the collar had been through many washes and had become 'frayed' after starching the stiff fibres became akin to a saw and chafed the neck – so one sat as still as possible!

33   This 1913 postcard shows the outside of the fourth side of the quadrangle which forms Cobham College – it is the refectory. The chantry (or endowment) was founded in 1363 by King Edward III. By Elizabeth the First's reign (1558) the college was a ruin. It had been in the possession of the Cobhams for generations, then by the will of Sir William Brooke, Lord Cobham in 1597 it was rebuilt, to be called the New College of Cobham, as almshouses for the poor. Could the 'lopsided' porch be part of the first building?

34   Here is a view of the 'backs' of the cottages above the 'Rose & Crown' on Butchers Hill. It would seem that domestic conditions were somewhat primitive compared with 1995. Of course, renovations have been done and apart from some features like window positions and a tidy garden, there would be some difficulty in recognising the place.

35   This is the view from the garden at the back of the 'Rose & Crown'. Very little has changed since the 1920's when this was recorded except that with the increased use of the motor car and social changes which include more 'eating out', a car park became essential and one was provided here in a space at the right hand of this picture.

36   The 'off' licence and bakery at Upper Bush was kept by Mr. Henry Baker and he is seen here photographed at the well in the early part of the century. The name of the brewery that supplied him with 'ale' was Dampiers of Strood; before this, beer was brewed on the premises. At the time of the picture there were 22 houses in the hamlet – no more than half a dozen now remain.

37 This postcard of the New College Almshouses at Cobham has the date stamp 1911 and shows one corner of the quadrangle which encloses the houses. In the past, each house was allocated for use by the villages which were subject to the influence of the Cobhams or their successors, namely, Cobham, 2 nominated poor; Shorne, 2; Cooling 1; Strood, 2; Hoo, 3; Higham, 1 and St Mary's, 1. If there were no names offered, then the following villages were offered places in a particular order, viz – Cliffe; Chalk; Gravesend and Cuxton. In recent years the houses have been refurbished but their external appearance is essentially the same as shown. The tall gentleman on the right hand standing in front of the window is reputed to be the great-great-grandfather of the gentleman who loaned the card.

38   Pupils anywhere in the same period look alike; only relatives, close friends or class-mates could identify the individuals. Miss Day is standing at the back, left, the other teacher is not known. Among the youngsters Ken Ashley is playing the drum; one wonders why he in particular should be known. As a schoolmaster, I am intrigued by the horticultural display and the enterprising 'nippers' who secured for themselves the comfortable seat.

39   This is a postcard view of Church Street, Cliffe, in the early 1920's. The photographer seems to have created some interest if the curiosity of the ladies brought them to their front doors, or they came out to enjoy the weather. The village policeman was there to supervise the 'traffic' – or to see if the horse 'droppings' were ready for collecting to put around his rose trees. The two carts outside the shop on the right had probably completed a delivery. The legs of a horse are just discernible behind the nearest cart whose shafts are empty. The 'Victoria' public house on the right figures in another picture. The last known occupant of the sunshaded shop on the right was 'Par-kers' and it was followed by a restaurant with the name 'Wilkies'.

40 Here is a group of primary school pupils in 1938 at Cuxton School; they are made up of the two lower classes. Back row, left to right: 1. Neville Allcorn; 2. Neil Thorpe; 3. Dudley Brown; 4. ?; 5. Raymond Blackwell; 6. Raymond Weaver; 7. Derek Church; 8. ?. Middle Row: 1. Marjorie Palmer; 2. ?. 3. ?; Michael Cook; 5. Eric Jarvis; 6. Peter Bond; 7. ?; 8. Rita Blackman; 9. ?. Front row: 1. Alice Eddington; 2. Margaret Clifton; 3. Thelma Hanchett; 4. Lorna Hanchett; 5. ?; 6. Ann Saunders; 7. Iris Taylor; 8. Roddy Bennywell; 9. Pamela Richmond; 10. Josey Verrall; 11. ?; 12. ?; 13. Dorothy Rabbitt.

41   At Church Street, near the church of St. Mary the Virgin in Lower Higham stands the Clerk's House and what used to be 'The Sun' Inn. The Inn was sold and the Clerk's House has been renovated to look as one imagines it did in the late seventeenth century. It is still thatched.

42   The White Hart farmhouse is a typical 'Whealden' house, one of several in the county. Unfortunately, the best of it is hidden under a layer of plaster. At the time when the picture was taken it was divided into cottages, otherwise the entrances would not be visible in these positions.

43   This picture shows Cuxton Station (Southern Railway Co) in 1870 or thereabouts, and shows the station master Mr. Cook, complete with top hat standing, proudly, in charge of his railway station. The station master held down a much respected position in any village and Mr. Cook was no exception. The station was considered to be Tudor in style: it was opened in 1856. The unusual double arm signals were the ground frame which were replaced in later years. The engine standing at the station platform was, in all probability a 'Cudworth' 2-4-0 built by Stirling for the South Eastern Railway Company. Mr. Cook installed a battery operated lighting system in his office and home, which was nearby. During the increasing use of batteries for operating the increasingly popular wireless, Mr. Cook was able to recharge batteries for the villagers and this he continued as a profitable business after retirement.

44   This postcard, dated 1925, is a picture of the filling station at Cliffe Woods about half a mile toward Rochester on the B2000. It was rebuilt during the 1960's and is now part of a large urban development which seems to have engulfed it. It is unlikely that the petrol brands are now available. For those of us who could have been present in this scene, the rear view of the vehicles is not unfamiliar and in those days we would talk of mudguards rather than 'wings', which were unheard of except on birds and aeroplanes.

45   This old postcard shows Church Hill, Cuxton, before 1921. The road to the right hand, which is now the driveway up to the church, was originally the road to Halling. The road on which the horse and 'trap' appears was the turnpike, constructed in 1827. The present day road follows this same line but there are houses on each side and it is much wider to accommodate a very large increase in traffic.

46   This is Wood Street, off Bush Road in October 1919. On the bread wagon is Rhoda Baker on her way around her customers. In the immediate background is the recreation ground, the 'Rec' and further up the hillside a field known as 'six acres'. There must be hundreds of thousands of houses up and down the country like this row, cut off from the street by a plaster-topped wall and good, solid, iron railings.

47   This postcard picture is of Halling High Street and is self-explanatory, in the 1920's. Traffic, as in so many places, began to cause congestion on the roads and this street provided notably difficult problems in the 1960's, 70's and 80's so that in the end a by-pass was provided and the village street is almost as quiet as when this picture was taken.

48 This is a view of the Rochester Road Cuxton early in this century. The White House Farm is on the left (referred to later) and below it can be seen the narrow entrance to Bush Road; it has been redesigned and enlarged since then. The White Hart public house is on the right, by now, redeveloped and, of course, provided with a car park. The notice leaning against the fence points the way to the 'S.E. and C.R. Cuxton Station' – another, later picture refers.

49   Here is a postcard showing The Street Cuxton, in 1906. The Street was later named Bush Road as it is today. It is recorded that there had been a slight sprinkling of snow. Opposite the row of houses was a hop garden. A new parish council, elected in 1898 was urged to provide street lighting, which it did, and one of the oil lamps is seen on the right. The only problem with the oil lamps was that the flame was frequently blown out in windy conditions and then the lamp-lighter had more than he could cope with. The lamps were extinguished each night after the last train had arrived at Cuxton Station.

The Street, Cuxton.

50   The left hand of this row of houses was Cuxton's first Post Office. The road was very narrow in the early part of the century but the acute corner has long since been straightened out. The flint walls on both sides of the road and the end wall of the terrace were typical of the period in this area. One item of note is the roof 'overhang' above the protruding window of the upper room.

51 William Shakespeare refers to Gads Hill and its relationship to robbery in Henry IV part I and he would have been aware of the Inn and its association with the young Prince Henry and his henchman and friend Sir John Falstaff. As far back as 1558, there was a ballad entitled 'the Robbers of Gads Hill' and it was famous for travellers being robbed on their journeys to Rochester, where stood the only bridge across the Medway below Aylesford on the main route to Dover and the continent, hence 'good pickings'. The 'Sir John Falstaff' stood at the top of a steep, thickly wooded hill and ideally suited the activities of highwaymen. The most famous of them was probably 'Swift Nick', a name given to him by King Charles II on hearing of his activities. His story is said to be the basis of the legend of Dick Turpin's famous ride to York on Black Bess. The picture shows the Inn about 1900. The horse and trap were familiar on the roads then and harnessed to a light 'trotting' horse, they were a comparatively fast mode of transport for short journeys and were much favoured by doctors.

52   This picture of the 'Sir John Falstaff' inn is of a similar period to the previous one – the difference is one of season as can be seen by the shape of the tree silhouettes. The main points of interest are focussed in the modes of transport. The open-topped bus might be of historical interest too, as it would seem to me that its tyres are probably among the earliest pneumatic variety and the rear wheels are in pairs. Most buses at this period were still shod in solid rubber. The other vehicle was probably a 'carrier's' cart of which many could be found on rural roads carrying goods of all kinds and sometimes passengers. Close to the wall another horse stands waiting.

53   This postcard of the 'Darnley Arms', bears the name of one of the families who occupied Cobham Hall. Very few alterations have been made to this Inn. Dated 1910, this postcard advertises Meux & Co's Beers and Stouts. The board at the gable end offers 'horses' and 'stabling'. The stone at the corner of the building is still there, smaller but wearing the scars of many encounters with the steel 'tyres' of carriage wheels. It is said that this building is older than the Leather Bottle but not as old as the Leather Bottle Cottage.

54   It is thought that this picture of 'The Chequers' Inn was taken about 1895, shortly before it was pulled down and replaced by the new building which stands at the junction of Buckland Lane and the road, Church Lane. I am puzzled by the tall structure in front of the chimney.

55 The 'Leather Bottle' Cobham, is seen here from a 'tinted' postcard published and 'supplied free exclusively by Shurey's Publications' about 1910. This is how the Inn appeared before all of the outer shell of plaster had been removed and the present day 'olde worlde' appearance had been provided. The vehicles appear to be in the style of the Irish 'jaunting carts' and the picture suggests that perhaps the landlord of the day had them there ready for hire. A leather bottle is hanging from the end of the curved sign board but is almost obscured by the dark side of the neighbouring house.

56   The 'Rose & Crown' stands on Butcher's Hill, the well-known centre of Shorne. The roadway level has been raised somewhat during much resurfacing and the mansard styled lean-to has been replaced. The 'Shrimp Brand Beers' are unknown in the area nowadays. The hostelry is a popular venue.

57   Here is a coach outing in the early part of the century, meeting outside the 'Victoria' public house, Church Street. The mode of transport would have been typical in those days as would the headgear of the participants – but only three of the men are wearing 'bowler' hats and one of them, number six on the front row, was John Couzins, related to the donor of the postcard.

58   Here, Halling firemen are about to start a race for the annually offered cup, which took place in the recreation ground. Those taking part were, left to right: Captain Brake and firemen Jennings; Wooden, Chittenden and one other. This event took place in 1930. The firemen are equipped with the basic items, standard at the time, of boots, helmet and axe and of course, the uniform. The Fire Brigades Act of 1938 transferred fire fighting responsibility to District Councils so, therefore, the locally supported fire brigades disappeared.

59   Here, we see the first three placings at Halling Athletics Sports Day in 1907. The mudguards had been discarded and also the brakes; the wheels look somewhat lighter in weight than standard but no special gearing is apparent.

60   This is another picture taken at the celebrations which were laid on for the Coronation of King George V at Cuxton. These young ladies were part of the procession seen in an earlier picture. Here can be seen two or three Union Jacks. The lady in the background, I would think a teacher, is having to secure her hat. I wonder what the little girl, looking in the direction of the camera is thinking about. Most of the girls are carrying handbags, and one, at least is well prepared with a mug.

61   The coronation of George V was celebrated in style and the centre of events was in the 'Rec'. Here is seen a procession of schoolchildren, led by a band (what happened to the boys?). The houses on the right were probably at the top end of Wood Street; the path in the foreground continued into 'six acre' field. In the left hand back corner of the picture is the school and the road in the centre is Bush Road with the elms providing a background.

62   The May Day procession was at one time an annual event and here is the scene in 1910 when the procession was passing along Kent Road. Leading the band are the members of Halling Council, followed by quite a number of the general public. It is a pity that the inscription on the banner is not readable – it was large and needed support on poles at each side and by ropes at each corner. The road was also decorated by bunting strung from houses on both sides.

63   This picture was taken outside the White Hart, Cuxton, in about 1920. The buildings seen here, the public house and the outbuildings have been replaced to provide better accomodation and the ever increasing use of the personal motor carriage. My impression is that, far from being a 'service' coach on the route, say, to Rochester, this was a novelty outing organised, perhaps, by Masons the Brewer.

64 A.P.C.M. (Associated Portland Cement Manufacturers) appeared to employ both weight and brawn and needed to, not only to become champions but also to do the hard work needed in the factory. Unfortunately, neither the names of these worthy gentlemen nor the venue for this picture are known.

65   The fire service at Cuxton was formed after the First World War and prior to that Rochester Fire Brigade had to be summoned and with a horse-drawn fire engine a long time elapsed between being summoned and arrival at the scene. Eventually, the Parish Council acquired a hand-cart, standpipe and hoses. The cart and equipment was stored on a plot of land where shops now occupy the site. Their first captain was a Mr. Sparrow. By the time the picture was taken, between the wars, the Brigade had acquired their personal equipment and, it seems, a championship cup.

66 This was the Rectory built in 1831 by Mr. Whitehead of Maidstone for Rector Robert Shaw. It replaced the old Rectory which was on Bush Road, probably on the site now occupied by the Scout hut. This building was of wattle and daub construction, very low lying and very damp, so much so in fact, that the few rectors who did live in it usually complained of suffering the most common ailment of the period, ague. One rector tried to make the place more habitable and had a layer of bricks placed on the outside walls. As it happened, most of the rectors lived elsewhere, usually in Rochester. The rectory of Robert Shaw was built of yellow brick and had a blue slate roof. It was in the late Georgian style but whilst it was an elegent building the size of the property as a whole became inappropriate for its usage and expensive to run and maintain — it was sold in 1965 and was replaced by the present building.

67   Shorne (or Sornes as it was known at the time of Domesday) was the original seat of the Cobham family and Henry the first Baron Cobham has an effigy in this church. It is dedicated to St. Peter and St. Paul and contains examples of several different architectural styles: Saxon; Norman; Early English; Decorated and Perpendicular. It also contains an interesting fifteenth century octagonal font. The construction is of Kent ragstone and flint. At one time there were roses over the porch.

68   The church of St. Peter and St. Paul at Shorne stands in the centre of the village in a long hollow in the side of a hill. On the south side the ground gradually rises to Shorne Ridgeway with its row of quaint old houses. On the north side the ground rises again to the picturesque post office, where there is a splended view of the River Thames.

69   This postcard was postmarked 1916 to an address in Fulham. Apart from the gates which no longer exist, the church has not been altered. Cobham College is out of sight, behind it. This is a large parish church and contains a large number of 'brasses' – bearing the effigy of many of the families who tenanted the Hall. One Cobham, Thomas, is buried in St. Werburgh's church in Hoo under a brass dated 1467, with his wife, Matilda. Standing high just inside the gateway is a memorial cross dedicated to the sixth Earl Darnley.

70   This picture of the 'new' church of St. John was taken about 1901 and shows the church, when built in 1862. It was built because of the increase in population in Upper Higham as compared with the area around St. Mary's, or Church Street as it was known. The Reverend Joseph Hindle, a wealthy man, recognised the need for another church and had St. John's built. Several alterations and additions have been made, including a new vestry. The old choir stalls were transferred to St. Marys and new oak ones were put in. On 1st July 1944 a flying bomb damaged the east end and chancel – repairs were completed in 1951.

71   This is the eastern end of St. Mary the Virgin looking out into and across the marshes. The trees on the right hide the track which continues for about 56 yards and then diverts from its line into a farmyard which is close to and may be part of the site of the old priory. The short, shingled spire at the western end of the northerly of the twin roofs can be seen. The wall at the eastern end containing twin windows forms a large letter M. The marsh here is crossed from east to west by a railway line. It is probable that a causeway continued along the line of this view and out into the Thames to facilitate the passage of a ferry crossing to the Essex coast. Some think that a ford, or the causeway did the whole crossing but that the importance of it declined in the thirteenth century as the result of tidal changes or exceptionally strong or violent storms.

72 The church of St. James at Cooling, seen here, is a 'redundant' church with no congregation and is the responsibility of the Church Commissioners to maintain. Parts of the nave date back to the Norman era as does the font. There are six twelfth century – and impressive – oak benches on the western side. Cooling has been described as 'the capital of English Lollardry' because of its association with Sir John Oldcastle.

73   In the churchyard of St. James, Cooling, can be found these lozenge-shaped gravestones, thirteen in number. They mark the graves of the children of the Comport family. All reference to the children suggests that they were all under two years old at the time of death. The cause of death is thought to have been marsh fever, ague, or something similar to malaria. The river Thames is two miles distant and all of marshy, low-lying ground. It is thought that Charles Dickens had this churchyard in mind when writing 'Great Expectations'.

74 The modern name of Cliffe has developed out of several others, from Clive in ancient records, sometimes 'Clovesho', (Cliffe at Hoo) and Bishops Clive. Hasted's description reads – 'The church, which stands at the north west side of Church Street is a large, handsome building, equal to most in this county. It consists of two side aisles, a nave and a chancel, all lofty and spacious; the roof is covered with lead and the walls embattled; at the west end is a good tower, in which is a clock and a ring of six bells. … In the chancel … are … six stalls for the use of the monks of Christ Church, Canterbury when they come to visit. … There was formally an organ in this church the case of which is yet remaining.' Who could describe it better?

Cliffe Church near Rochester.

75 This postcard shows the interior of Cliffe church; it is the only church in Kent dedicated to St. Helen and is among the largest parish churches in Kent. It was built about 1260 in alternating bands of Kent ragstone and squared black flints. The nave is 100 feet long and the transepts are 82 feet north to south. The size of the church would indicate the importance of St. Helen's Church in earlier centuries; in fact in medieval times before the building of the present stone church, and it is believed that important synods were held here or hereabouts. The beautifully carved pulpit is worthy of note. The rood screen was removed in 1681 by rector and puritan George Groom.

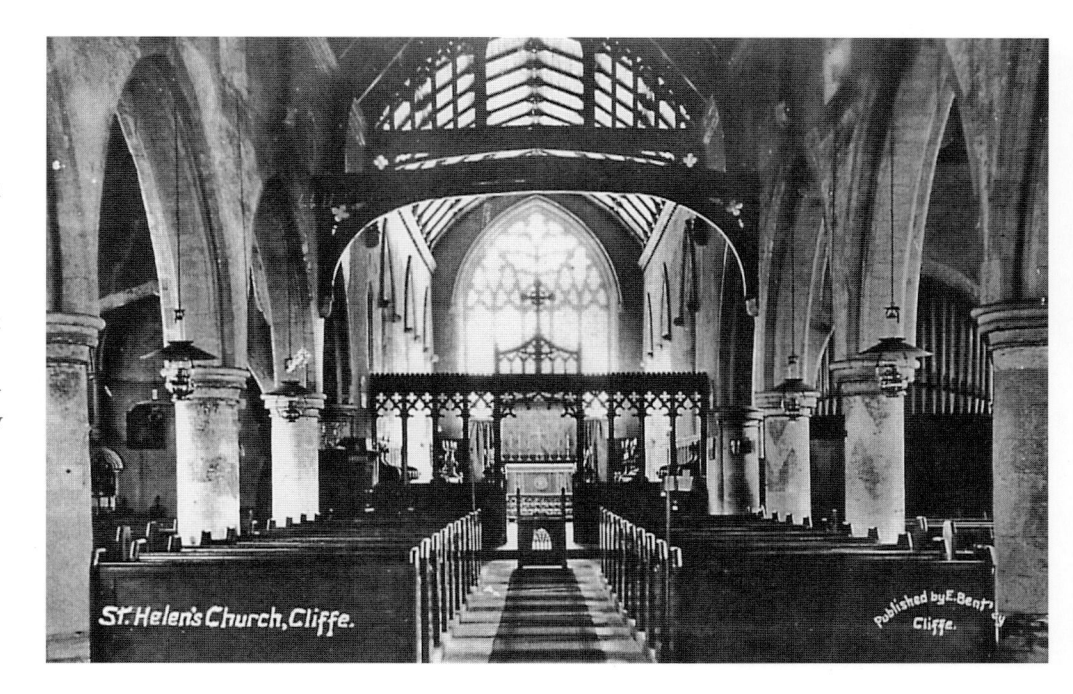

76   The Larkin memorial was put up on Telegraph Hill, the highest part of Higham, in 1835. It is in memory of Charles Larkin (1775-1833), a Rochester auctioneer. He introduced parliamentary reform which gave the vote to the occupants of every house with a rental value of more than £10. He was a prominent politician and known throughout the country. A local newspaper described the monument as follows: 'It is a column nearly sixty feet in height, built of a composition called concrete, in imitation of stone.' By August, 1860, the same newspaper reported, 'The Larkin Monument ... erected of concrete ... is found to be in peril of tumbling into a heap of rubbish.' It was repaired in 1869 with an inscription explaining that it had been repaired.